D0771058

LIGHTNING BOLT BOOKS™

Let's Visit the Evergreen Forest

Buffy Silverman

Lerner Publications • Minneapolis

Lerner Publications Company
A division of Lerner Publishing Group, Inc.
241 First Avenue North
Minneapolis, MN 55401 USA

For reading levels and more information, look up this title at www.lernerbooks.com.

Library of Congress Cataloging-in-Publication Data

Names: Silverman, Buffy.
Title: Let's visit the evergreen forest / Buffy Silverman.
Description: Minneapolis : Lerner Publications, 2016. | Series: Lightning bolt books. Biome explorers |
    Audience: Ages 5–8. | Audience: K to Grade 3. | Includes bibliographical references and index.
Identifiers: LCCN 2015048772 (print) | LCCN 2016009923 (ebook) | ISBN 9781512411911 (lb : alk. paper)
    | ISBN 9781512412291 (pb : alk. paper) | ISBN 9781512411997 (eb pdf)
Subjects: LCSH: Forest ecology—Juvenile literature. | Conifers—Ecology—Juvenile literature. |
    Evergreens--Juvenile literature.
Classification: LCC QH541.5.F6 S56 2016 (print) | LCC QH541.5.F6 (ebook) | DDC 577.3—dc23

LC record available at http://lccn.loc.gov/2015048772

Manufactured in the United States of America
1 - 39693 - 21304 - 3/28/2016

Table of Contents

A Journey to the Evergreen Forest

Imagine hiking through an evergreen forest. Tall trees tower above you. Their needles carpet the ground. Their scent fills the air.

Snow blankets this habitat in winter. It covers trees. This makes it hard for animals to travel and find food.

The evergreen forest biome stretches across Alaska and Canada. It also covers parts of northern Europe and Asia.

NORTH
AMERICA

EUROPE

ASIA

AFRICA

SOUTH
AMERICA

AUSTRALIA

Evergreen forest

ANTARCTICA

Days are very short during winter in the evergreen forest. The temperature stays below freezing for many months.

Summers are cool in an evergreen forest. The ground is wet and swampy. The days are long.

Plants grow quickly during the short summer. Insects hatch. Birds feast on insects. The forest comes to life.

Animals in the Forest

Animals in an evergreen forest must survive snowy winters. A snowshoe hare's fur turns white. White fur helps it stay hidden in the snow.

Lynx and other predators sometimes spot a hare. The hare leaps away. Its large, furry feet keep it from sinking in snow.

An elk grows a thick coat for winter. Its winter coat is five times warmer than its summer coat. It steps through deep snow with its long legs.

This elk has grown its thick, warm winter coat.

Voles tunnel beneath soil and snow. Five or more voles nest together in winter. They huddle together to stay warm. They eat roots belowground.

A red fox can hear a vole under the snow 25 feet (7.6 meters) away.

A red fox listens for voles. He tilts his ears. He leaps and dives into the snow. The fox scoops up his prey.

Insects hatch in swampy forest pools in summer. Mosquitoes quickly grow into adults. They mate and lay their eggs before winter begins. The eggs hatch when summer returns.

Many birds nest in the evergreen forest. They catch insects to feed their young. They fly south before winter.

This warbler can fly about 5,000 miles (8,050 kilometers) to reach its nesting ground.

A pine grosbeak usually lives
in the evergreen forest all
year. Its thick bill crushes
seeds. It finds fruit on bushes.

Plants in the Forest

Spruce, fir, pine, and hemlock trees grow in an evergreen forest. They have green needles all year. Needles are leaves. Needles usually fall off a tree after a few years.

Evergreen needles can make
food for the tree as soon as
the weather gets warm. The
dark needles absorb sunlight.

Needles are thin and waxy. They help the tree save water in winter.

These needles absorb light, save water, and do not freeze in winter.

Evergreen tree branches droop down. Heavy snow slips off the branches. It slides off the waxy needles.

Thick mats of moss grow in evergreen forests. Moss plants do not have roots. Their leaves and stems fill with water. They hold in water like a sponge.

Lichens often grow on rocks, trees, or stumps.

Lichens also grow in the evergreen forest. Lichens are made of algae and fungi. Green algae make food. Fungi get water from the air. They give algae shade.

Living in the Forest

Animals in a forest ecosystem depend on plants for survival. Mice and birds eat seeds. Moose eat buds and twigs. Insects chew wood and needles.

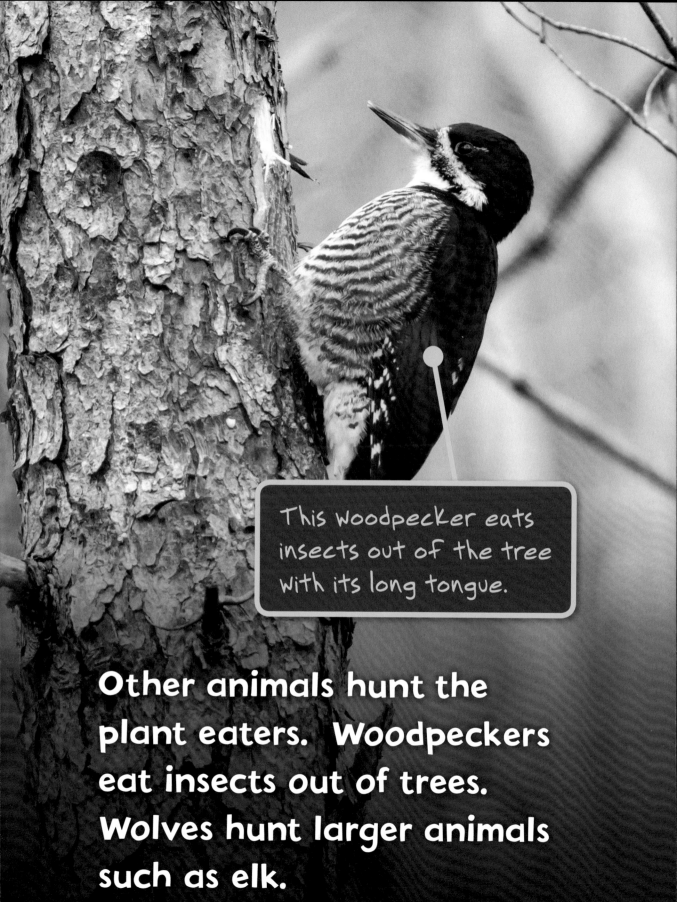

This woodpecker eats insects out of the tree with its long tongue.

Other animals hunt the plant eaters. Woodpeckers eat insects out of trees. Wolves hunt larger animals such as elk.

Soil forms slowly in the cold, wet forest. It gets nutrients from dead plants and animals. The soil is thin and freezes in winter. Only certain plants can grow in this soil.

Living things help make soil. Woodpeckers drill into dead trees. The trees fall to the ground. Small animals, fungi, and bacteria break down the wood. Plants and animals depend on one another in the evergreen forest biome.

People in the Evergreen Forest

People have lived in the evergreen forest for thousands of years. But most of the region has few people, so there are not many cities in this biome. Some people herd reindeer in the evergreen forests of Russia. They fish in summer and hunt in winter.

Most people in the evergreen forest live a modern life. People drill for oil and gas there. They log trees. The wood is used to make paper. Mining, drilling, and logging can harm forests. Some people replant trees that are logged. They also pass laws and make plans to keep forests safe.

Biome Extremes

- **Coldest winters:** northeastern Russia (−65°F, or −54°C)

- **Largest cat:** Siberian tiger, from eastern Russia

- **Biggest browser:** moose (1,800 pounds, or 816 kilograms)

- **World's largest wetland:** found in Canada's evergreen forest

- **Largest land biome:** evergreen forest, 29 percent of the world's forests

Glossary

algae: plantlike living creatures that usually grow in water

biome: a community where certain plants and animals live, such as a desert or forest

ecosystem: a group of connected living and nonliving things

evergreen: a plant that has green leaves throughout the entire year

fungi: organisms such as mushrooms that break down dead plants and animals.

habitat: the natural home of plants or animals

lichen: an organism made of fungi and algae living together

needle: a finely pointed leaf of a tree

nutrient: a substance that plants, animals, and people need to live and grow

predator: an animal that kills and eats other animals

Further Reading

Biomes of the World: Taiga
http://www.mbgnet.net/sets/taiga/index
.htm

The Boreal Forest Is Where I Want to Be
https://www.youtube.com/watch?v=DEewbMP2zOY

Felix, Rebecca. *What's Great about Alaska?*
Minneapolis: Lerner Publications, 2016.

Fleisher, Paul. *Forest Food Webs in Action.*
Minneapolis: Lerner Publications, 2014.

Johansson, Philip. *The Taiga: Discover This
Forested Biome.* Berkeley Heights, NJ: Enslow
Elementary, 2015.

Messner, Kate. *Over and under the Snow.* San
Francisco: Chronicle Books, 2011.

World Biomes: Taiga
http://kids.nceas.ucsb.edu/biomes/taiga.html

Index

Photo Acknowledgments

The images in this book are used with the permission of: © Nature Photographers Ltd/ Alamy, p. 2; © Chromakey/Shutterstock.com, p. 4; © iStockphoto.com/naumoid, p. 5; © Laura Westlund/Independent Picture Service, p. 6; © iStockphoto.com/ ahansenoutdoors, p. 7; © Denise Lett/Shutterstock.com, p. 8; © iStockphoto.com/ georgeolsson, p. 9; © MVPhoto/Shutterstock.com, pp. 10, 11, 25; © iStockphoto.com/ PaulTessier, p. 12; © Michael S. Quinton/Getty Images, p. 13; © Stock Connection Blue/ Alamy, p. 14; © iStockphoto.com/stillwords, p. 15; © Nature Photographers Ltd/Alamy, p. 16; © David Tipling/Alamy, p. 17; © iStockphoto.com/Alexander Gatsenko, p. 18; © 3355m/Shutterstock.com, p. 19; © Aleksey Stemmer/Shutterstock.com, p. 20; © Dmytro Kosmenko/Shutterstock.com, p. 21; © mrivserg/Shutterstock.com, p. 22; © Robert Cicchetti/Shutterstock.com, p. 23; © George Grall/Getty Images, p. 24; © Yu Sui Kao/Shutterstock.com, p. 26; © Andrew F. Kazmierski/Shutterstock.com, p. 27; © Howard Sandler/Shutterstock.com, p. 31.

Front cover: © Barrett Hedges/National Geographic/Getty Images

Main body text set in Johann Light 30/36.